Cornerstones of Freedom

The United Nations

R. Conrad Stein

CHILDRENS PRESS®

CHICAGO

Library of Congress Cataloging-in-Publication Data

Stein, R. Conrad.
  The United Nations / by R. Conrad Stein.
    p. cm. – (Cornerstones of freedom)
  ISBN 0-516-06677-3
  1. United Nations–Juvenile literature.
[1. United Nations.] I. Title. II. Series.
JX1977.Z8S795 1994
341.23–dc20   93-37030
[B]   CIP
                                                        AC

In the fall of 1962, President John F. Kennedy received a report that the Russians were installing medium-range ballistic missiles in Cuba. To investigate the claim, the president ordered United States reconnaissance planes on a secret photography mission. The planes came back with remarkably clear pictures. Now there were no doubts. The Soviet Union, trying to gain a quick advantage over the United States in the delicate balance of power, was placing offensive missiles in Cuba, just ninety miles from U.S. soil.

On October 22, 1962, President Kennedy gave a chilling speech over national television that those who were watching will never forget. He told the world that he had ordered the U.S. Navy

The U2 plane, used by the U.S. military to photograph Russian missiles in Cuba

President Kennedy informs the nation about the Cuban Missile Crisis.

to "quarantine" all Soviet ships heading toward Cuba. This meant that American warships would stop Soviet freighters, board them, and search them for missiles before allowing the ships to proceed. If the Soviet ships refused to stop, they would be fired on and possibly sunk. The American president had issued a deadly challenge to the Russians. The two nations were inches away from a devastating nuclear war.

On October 25, the drama of the Cuban Missile Crisis shifted to the United Nations building in New York City. Speaking before the Security Council, the U.S. ambassador, Adlai Stevenson, demanded that the Soviets remove their missiles from Cuba at once. Soviet Ambassador Valerian

Photographs from the U.S. spy planes (left) revealed the Russian missiles on Cuban soil. A political cartoon (right) portrayed the standoff between the Soviet Union and the United States.

Tensions run high at the UN as Stevenson (right) challenges Zorin (left) to deny the existence of Soviet missiles in Cuba.

Zorin at first implied that there were no Russian missiles on the island. Stevenson, growing angry, said, "Do you, Ambassador Zorin, deny that the USSR has placed and is placing medium- and intermediate-range missiles and sites in Cuba? Yes or no?"

The Soviet ambassador listened through earphones while a United Nations translator related Stevenson's question in Russian. But Stevenson believed that Zorin had understood his question, and he shouted out, "Don't wait for the translation. Yes or no?"

Finally, Zorin said he would answer the question "in due course."

"I am prepared to wait for my answer until hell freezes over," Stevenson replied.

UN Secretary-General U Thant helped settle the missile crisis before it came to war.

As the debate raged, the United Nations secretary-general, U Thant, quietly offered compromise proposals to the two feuding nations. Finally, after endless hours of tense negotiations, it was agreed that the Soviet Union would remove its missiles, and the Cubans would allow a UN inspection team to visit the island to make sure the missiles were gone.

The Cuban Missile Crisis was over. With help from the United Nations, the world had perhaps been saved from nuclear war. The UN's role as a peacemaker during the crisis was a fulfillment of its founders' dreams.

The United Nations was born during a war in the hope of preventing future wars. Late in World War II, the Allied powers sought to create an organization to keep the peace after the war ended. The Allies dreamed of forming a large assembly of nations that would provide peaceful methods of settling disputes.

The idea of a worldwide alliance for peace was not new. At the end of World War I, an organization called the League of Nations was established. The League of Nations had the same major goal as the present-day United Nations. The member nations hoped to resolve international problems in a peaceful manner.

One of the most enthusiastic supporters of the League of Nations was American president

Below: A 1919 political cartoon expressing some skepticism that the new League of Nations would be able to maintain worldwide peace Right: A 1932 session of the League of Nations

Woodrow Wilson. But, in the United States, all treaties must be ratified by the Senate. The American Senate refused to let the president sign the treaty that would make the United States a member of the League of Nations. The main reason for the Senate's action was a mood of isolationism that swept the country after World War I. At the time, many people felt that the United States should separate—or isolate—itself from problems arising elsewhere in the world.

The League of Nations lasted a little more than twenty years. It was, for the most part, an ineffective body. Before World War II, a number of skirmishes broke out that the league was unable to stop. In 1935, Italy invaded Ethiopia. Later, a bloody civil war erupted in Spain. Then, in 1939, Germany attacked Poland, the League of Nations collapsed, and the world plunged into the most costly war in history.

World War II began when German forces invaded Poland in 1939.

The League of Nations failed as a peacekeeping body primarily because the United States was not a member. The United States had become the most powerful country of the twentieth century, and its absence doomed the old League of Nations from its start. But the lessons of World War II were too important to ignore. The war left millions dead and destroyed entire cities. Sensible people in the U.S. and elsewhere began to demand that a strong peacekeeping alliance of nations be established.

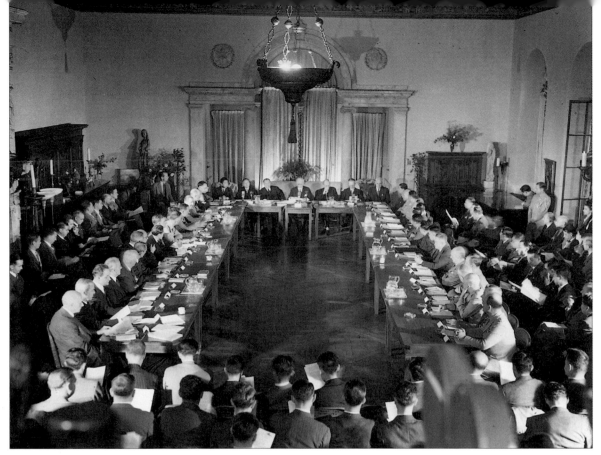

The 1944 Dumbarton Oaks Conference laid the groundwork for the formation of the United Nations.

On August 21, 1944, while World War II still raged, representatives of the United States, the Soviet Union, Great Britain, and China met at Dumbarton Oaks, a handsome old estate near Washington, D.C. Delegates to this Dumbarton Oaks Conference agreed to establish a new organization, to be called the United Nations (UN). On April 25, 1945, men and women of forty-six nations gathered at San Francisco to draft a charter for the new UN.

If any of the delegates still doubted the need for a worldwide peacekeeping body, their doubts

WE THE PEOPLES OF THE UNITED NATIONS DETERMINED

to save succeeding generations from the scourge of war, which twice in our lifetime has brought untold sorrow to mankind, and

to reaffirm faith in fundamental human rights, in the dignity and worth of the human person, in the equal rights of men and women and of nations large and small, and

to establish conditions under which justice and respect for the obligations arising from treaties and other sources of international law can be maintained, and

to promote social progress and better standards of life in larger freedom,

AND FOR THESE ENDS

to practice tolerance and live together in peace with one another as good neighbors, and

to unite our strength to maintain international peace and security, and

to ensure, by the acceptance of principles and the institution of methods, that armed force shall not be used, save in the common interest, and

to employ international machinery for the promotion of the economic and social advancement of all peoples,

HAVE RESOLVED TO COMBINE OUR EFFORTS TO ACCOMPLISH THESE AIMS.

Accordingly, our respective Governments, through representatives assembled in the city of San Francisco, who have exhibited their full powers found to be in good and due form, have agreed to the present Charter of the United Nations and do hereby establish an international organization to be known as the United Nations.

Secretary of the U.S. Senate Leslie Biffle (above) signs the UN charter (right).

August 6, 1945: The atomic bomb is dropped on Hiroshima, Japan.

vanished on August 6, 1945. On that day, a single American bomber dropped a single atomic bomb, obliterating the Japanese city of Hiroshima. Clearly this terrible new weapon could destroy all life on earth. The United Nations was not only desirable, it was now vital.

On October 24, 1945, the new United Nations was born. Today that date is hailed as UN Day. In the United States, the old isolationist feelings had disappeared entirely. This time, the United States Senate chose to join the organization by an overwhelming vote of 89 to 2.

The founders of the United Nations drew up a charter to state the purpose and functions of the organization. The charter is similar to a country's constitution. The original charter listed four major aims the UN hoped to achieve: 1) to keep the peace, 2) to encourage nations to be just in their dealings with each other, 3) to promote cooperation between countries, and 4) to provide an agency where all nations can work together in harmony.

Keeping the peace is the most important goal of the UN. The first sentence of the charter reads, "We, the peoples of the United Nations, determined to save succeeding generations from the scourge of war which twice in our lifetime has brought untold sorrow to mankind." The UN's peacekeeping operations fall primarily on three separate bodies: the Security Council, the General Assembly, and the office of the secretary-general.

When the charter was written, the Security Council was viewed as the UN's major peacekeeping agency. Dominated by the large powers, it was to act as an international "police force" and send troops to restore peace in any of the world's trouble spots. It was hoped that the five major nations that won World War II—the United States, the Soviet Union, Great Britain, France, and China—would continue to work together on the Security Council.

But disagreements quickly developed among these great powers. Four years after the birth of

As this 1947 cartoon shows, some people had doubts that the UN would be able to control the rivalries between the world's superpowers.

Mao Zedong led the 1949 Communist revolution in China. For decades afterward, China's status in the UN was a point of controversy.

Delegates from the People's Republic of China take their UN seats for the first time in 1971.

the UN, a Communist revolution succeeded in China and the old Chinese government was forced to flee to the island of Taiwan. The United States wanted the deposed government to retain its seat on the Security Council, even though it now represented only a tiny minority of the Chinese people. The Soviets demanded that the new Communist government replace the old one. The U.S. and its allies won the initial dispute, and it was not until 1971 that Communist China was allowed to take a permanent seat on the Security Council. The squabble over the China question, however, weakened the effectiveness of the Security Council.

The Security Council is made up of fifteen member nations, five of which are called "permanent." The five permanent members are the United States, The Russian Federation, China, Great Britain, and France. Ten "temporary" members are elected for two-year terms by the UN as a whole. The rules state that any of the five permanent members can vote against, or veto, any action of the Security Council. For example, in 1950, Communist forces from North Korea invaded South Korea. The Security Council voted to send troops to repel the invasion. The Soviet Union certainly would have vetoed that action. But at the time, the Russian

The first meeting of the UN Security Council, March 25, 1946

Each UN member nation has one vote in the General Assembly.

delegation was boycotting the UN in protest over
the Security Council's refusal to seat Communist
China. Over the years, Russia has exercised its
veto in the Security Council more than one
hundred times.

The General Assembly is a worldwide congress.
It is the only body in the UN in which every
member nation has one vote. No single nation is
able to veto an act of the General Assembly. Its
powers as a peacekeeping body were greatly
enhanced in 1950, when it passed the "Uniting

for Peace" resolution. This resolution gave the General Assembly the authority to act on a dangerous situation when the Security Council is rendered powerless by vetoes.

An important function of the General Assembly is to provide a worldwide forum for nations that are either at war or on the brink of war. This kind of public debate was helpful in finding a peaceful solution during the dangerous Cuban Missile Crisis. Today, important sessions of the General Assembly can be carried via satellite to almost every television set in the world. Angry delegates sometimes exchange insults and curses on the floor of the General Assembly. Soviet Premier Nikita Khrushchev once took off his shoe and pounded it on the table to drive home a point during a General Assembly debate. But fiery words and gestures are always preferable to bombs and missiles.

Soviet Premier Nikita Khrushchev gestures emphatically while addressing the General Assembly in 1960.

The secretary-general is the chief administrator of the UN and could be thought of as its chairman or mayor. The secretary-general is nominated by the Security Council and is approved by a majority vote of the General Assembly. He or she serves a five-year term and can be reelected.

All five permanent members of the Security Council must agree on a candidate for the office before the name goes to the General Assembly for the final vote. To avoid giving an advantage to one of the major powers, the secretary-general is usually someone who is not from one of those nations.

The secretary-general is vital to the UN's peacekeeping functions. The charter authorizes him to advise the Security Council on any war-threatening situation. He has a similar role with the General Assembly. He also acts as a mediator in disputes between all powers, large or small. The secretary-general is more flexible in mediating disputes than is a large body such as the General Assembly, or a divided body such as the Security Council. Secretary-General U Thant helped mediate the Cuban Missile Crisis because his integrity had won the confidence of both the Soviets and the Americans.

Men of extraordinary ability have occupied the secretary-general's office. Trygve Lie of Norway, elected in 1946, was the UN's first secretary-

Trygve Lie　　　　*Dag Hammarskjöld*　　　　*Javier Pérez de Cuéllar*

general. One of the most revered secretaries-
general was Dag Hammarskjöld of Sweden, who
served from 1953 to 1961. He helped ease tensions
between the United States and the Soviet Union.
Hammarskjöld died in a 1961 plane crash while
on a UN mission to Africa. U Thant, a Burmese
diplomat, served from 1961 to 1972, when many
African and Asian countries were in chaos. Kurt
Waldheim of Austria served from 1972 to 1982.
He helped resolve a war in the Middle East.

Javier Pérez de Cuéllar of Peru succeeded
Waldheim and became the UN's fifth secretary-
general. His biggest accomplishment was
negotiating a cease-fire that ended the Iran-Iraq
war in 1989. In 1992, Egypt's Boutros Boutros-
Ghali became secretary-general. He was

Boutros Boutros-Ghali

immediately faced with such tasks as mediating a civil war that tore apart the former Yugoslavia, and providing humanitarian relief to victims of military fighting in Somalia. All the men who have held the office of secretary-general have been known for their intelligence, their energy, and above all, their fairness.

The other UN peacekeeping body is the International Court of Justice, also called the World Court. Its fifteen judges are chosen by the Security Council and the General Assembly. This court hears arguments from countries locked in a dispute and then makes a judgment. The dispute

Citizens of Somalia welcome UN peacekeeping troops.

The World Court is headquartered in The Hague, The Netherlands.

might be a disagreement over national boundaries or over fishing rights in the ocean. One weakness plaguing the court is that it has no way of enforcing its decisions. For example, in May 1980, the World Court ordered the revolutionary government of Iran to release the American hostages it captured during a raid on the U.S. embassy in Tehran. But the Iranian government ignored the order and held the people prisoner until January 1981.

Iranian terrorists who took Americans hostage in 1979

The UN's peacekeeping efforts have met with both successes and failures. In its fifty-year

A superpower was suddenly removed from world politics when the Soviet Union crumbled in 1991.

history it has never faced a conflict of the awesome magnitude of World War II. But the Vietnam War raged for years despite the UN's efforts to bring about a settlement. The UN was also powerless to prevent the 1982 Falkland Islands War between Argentina and Great Britain. On the other hand, the UN was able to arrange cease-fires in the complex and volatile Middle East when wars between Arabs and Israelis broke out there in 1967 and 1973.

The fall of the Soviet Union in 1991 changed the face of international politics. The world was no longer faced with two mighty powers—the Soviet Union and the United States—in constant disagreement and sometimes dangerously close to war. As these two superpowers lost their influence, many people wondered whether the United Nations would be able to control world peace.

The UN's first big challenge of the new era was the Persian Gulf conflict, which erupted when Iraq invaded neighbor Kuwait in 1990 to claim its rich oil fields. The UN authorized economic sanctions against Iraq—all UN member nations were told to stop doing business with Iraq. The purpose was to cripple the Iraqi economy until

On August 9, 1990, the UN Security Council voted unanimously against Iraq's claim on Kuwaiti territory.

After the 1991 Gulf War ended, a UN inspection team was sent to Iraq to make sure it complied with the terms of its surrender treaty. Here, inspectors examine an Iraqi chemical-weapon storage site.

its president, Saddam Hussein, gave in and withdrew from Kuwait. Hussein held firm, however, and his country managed to survive the UN's sanctions.

When this tactic failed, United States president George Bush organized an international army. In January 1991, with the UN's permission, a devastating military assault code-named Desert Storm was launched against Iraq, driving its forces out of Kuwait. Iraq eventually surrendered, but many lives had been lost. Despite the UN's efforts to obtain a peaceful solution, the situation ended in the most brutal military conflict the world had seen in years.

In the early 1990s, war erupted in such countries as Afghanistan, Ethiopia, Liberia, Somalia, Sudan, and the former Yugoslavia.

Because sophisticated, deadly weapons are easily available in the world today, these relatively small wars have inflicted immense suffering on innocent people.

These conflicts stem from complex disagreements that are often based on long-standing racial and ethnic prejudices. The UN has often found it impossible to either take sides or negotiate peace. It has, however, aggressively provided "humanitarian aid" to the thousands of victims of these bloody battles. Many UN soldiers

In 1993, UN troops were sent to deliver humanitarian aid to the people of Bosnia-Herzegovina, victims of a bloody civil war.

UN peacekeeping forces are made up of soldiers from many different nations.

have sacrificed their own lives in the effort to deliver food, medicine, and shelter to the citizens of these war-torn nations.

Intervention in wars is the most dramatic and publicized of all the UN's activities. But the organization's other efforts to improve the welfare of the world's people have achieved equally dramatic results.

One goal stated in the UN charter is to "promote social progress and better standards of life." To help give the world a better standard of living, the UN has created agencies staffed by technicians from all over the world. These technicians might be doctors, teachers, or farming experts. They are sent to underdeveloped countries where they introduce modern methods of growing food, combating disease, and teaching people to read. UN agencies have achieved some stunning triumphs in social welfare.

At one time, smallpox was the most deadly disease to affect mankind. Over its long and dark history, smallpox killed hundreds of millions of people and left many more permanently scarred and blinded. Vaccines were developed, and by the 1940s, the disease had been eliminated in Europe and North America. But smallpox still scourged Africa, Asia, and South America. In 1967, a UN agency called the World Health Organization (WHO) began a campaign to eradicate this

A UN soldier from Canada gives a checkup to a Cambodian child.

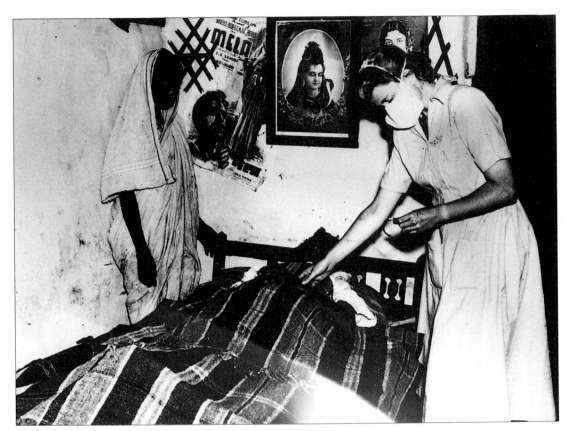

A World Health Organization nurse comes to the aid of a plague victim in India in 1950.

A WHO nurse checks an Angolan man for symptoms of sleeping sickness.

ancient plague forever. Health-care workers from WHO trekked into the tiniest villages in the remotest corners of the world. They vaccinated people and isolated those already afflicted. Because of their heroic efforts, only six cases of smallpox were reported anywhere on earth in 1973. In 1980, WHO announced that the curse of smallpox no longer existed. It was the first time in history that an organized human crusade had eradicated a disease from the planet.

The constitution of a UN agency called UNESCO starts with the words, "Since wars

UN representatives are often the first to arrive when war or famine strike in the Third World.

begin in the minds of men, it is in the minds of men that the defenses of peace must be constructed." UNESCO is the United Nations Educational, Scientific, and Cultural Organization. Established in 1946, the agency is headquartered in Paris, France. It encourages the work of artists, scientists, thinkers, and poets. One of its primary goals is to teach people in developing countries how to read. UNESCO trains teachers and provides books so that people from families that have been illiterate for generations can experience the joy of reading.

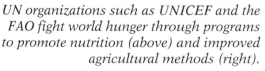

UN organizations such as UNICEF and the FAO fight world hunger through programs to promote nutrition (above) and improved agricultural methods (right).

In the 1970s, the populations of underdeveloped countries soared while their food production declined. The result was mass starvation. The major UN agency devoted to fighting hunger is the Food and Agriculture Organization (FAO), established in 1945. Farm experts from the FAO teach modern agriculture to farmers whose methods are outdated and therefore not as productive as they could be.

Some other UN agencies include:

- **General Agreement on Tariffs and Trade** (GATT)—sponsors trade negotiations between countries; established 1948
- **International Monetary Fund** (IMF)—promotes cooperation between countries in money affairs; established 1945

- **United Nations Childrens Fund** (UNICEF)—aids more than 100 nations to improve the health and education of children; established 1946
- **United Nations Industrial Development Organization** (UNIDO)—helps developing countries in money affairs; established 1966
- **Universal Postal Union** (UPU)—helps governments modernize and speed up mail systems; established 1947
- **World Meteorological Organization** (WMO)—helps developing countries establish their own weather bureaus; established 1950

United Nations headquarters in New York City

Today the glittering UN building in New York City is a favorite spot for groups of tourists and schoolchildren. The enormous meeting hall remains a unique assembly of nations. By 1994, the UN had grown to more than 180 member nations. Many of the members are small, developing countries that once were colonies of European powers. Others are countries that declared their independence when the Soviet Union splintered in 1991.

The United Nations does have its critics, but most people realize that it is our only form of world government. It is our best hope to prevent another world war.

President John F. Kennedy expressed this sentiment when he spoke before the General Assembly in 1961 and said, "Together we shall save our planet or together we shall perish in its flames. Save it we can, and save it we must, and then we shall earn the eternal thanks of mankind and, as peacemakers, the eternal blessing of God."

UN soldiers receive the highest payment of all: the smiles of children.

INDEX

PHOTO CREDITS

Cover, SuperStock International; 1, Wide World Photos; 2, SuperStock International; 3, Department of the Air Force; 4 (top), John F. Kennedy Library; 4 (bottom left), CIA; 4 (bottom right), © Richard Q. Yardley, *The Baltimore Sun*, Permission of Susan Yardley Wheltle; 5, 6, UPI/Bettmann; 7, Stock Montage, Inc.; 8, AP/Wide World; 9, UPI/Bettmann; 10 (top left), Stock Montage, Inc.; 10 (top right, bottom), UPI/Bettmann; 11, Stock Montage, Inc.; 12 (top), AP/Wide World; 12 (bottom), 13, UPI/Bettmann; 14, Wide World Photos; 15, 17, UPI/Bettmann; 18 (top), Wide World Photos; 18 (bottom), 19 (top), United Nations; 19 (bottom), 20, AP/Wide World; 21, Reuters/Bettmann; 22, United Nations; 23, Wide World Photos; 24, 25, United Nations; 26 (top), AP/Wide World; 26 (bottom), UPI/Bettmann; 27 (left), Reuters/Bettmann; 27 (right), United Nations; 28 (left), The Bettmann Archive; 28 (right), 29, United Nations; 30, Wide World Photos; 31, Reuters/Bettmann

Picture Identifications:
Cover: Flags of UN member nations in front of UN headquarters in New York City
Page 1: A session of the General Assembly
Page 2: The Secretariat Building and General Assembly Building of UN headquarters

Project Editor: Shari Joffe
Design: Karen Yops
Photo Research: Jan Izzo
Cornerstones of Freedom Logo: David Cunningham

ABOUT THE AUTHOR

R. Conrad Stein was born and raised in Chicago. He enlisted in the Marine Corps at the age of eighteen and served for three years. He then attended the University of Illinois, where he received a bachelor's degree in history. He later studied in Mexico, earning an advanced degree from the University of Guanajuato. Mr. Stein is the author of many books, articles, and short stories for young people.

Mr. Stein lives in Chicago with his wife and their daughter Janna.